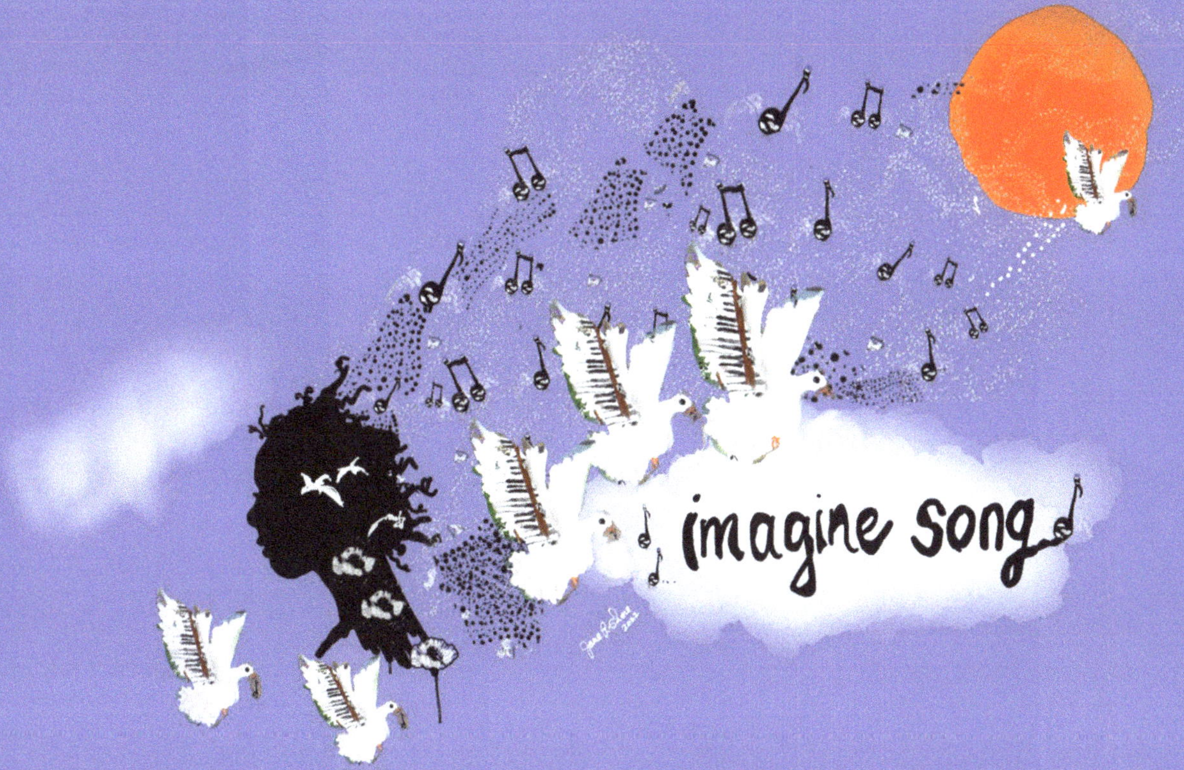
imagine song

Imagine Song

Published in the United States of America

ISBN Paperback: 978-1-959165-60-6
ISBN eBook: 978-1-959165-61-3

ReadersMagnet, LLC
10620 Treena Street, Suite 230 | San Diego, California, 92131 USA
1.619. 354. 2643 | www.readersmagnet.com

Cover design by Ericka Obando
Interior design by Daniel Lopez

A Story about the Kindred Connection between a Child, an Instrument, and an Imagination

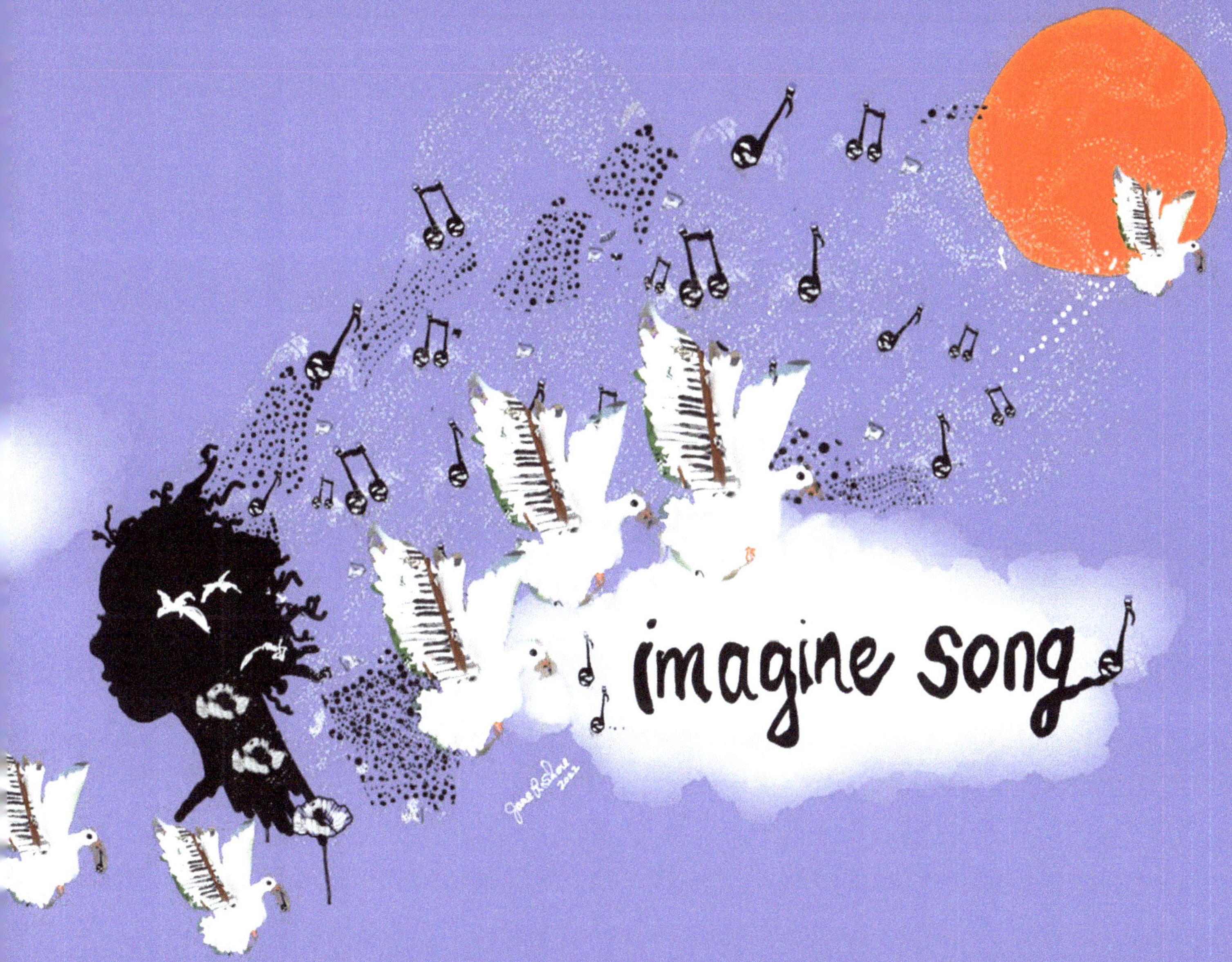

written by Melissa A. Campesi
illustrated by Jane R. Shore

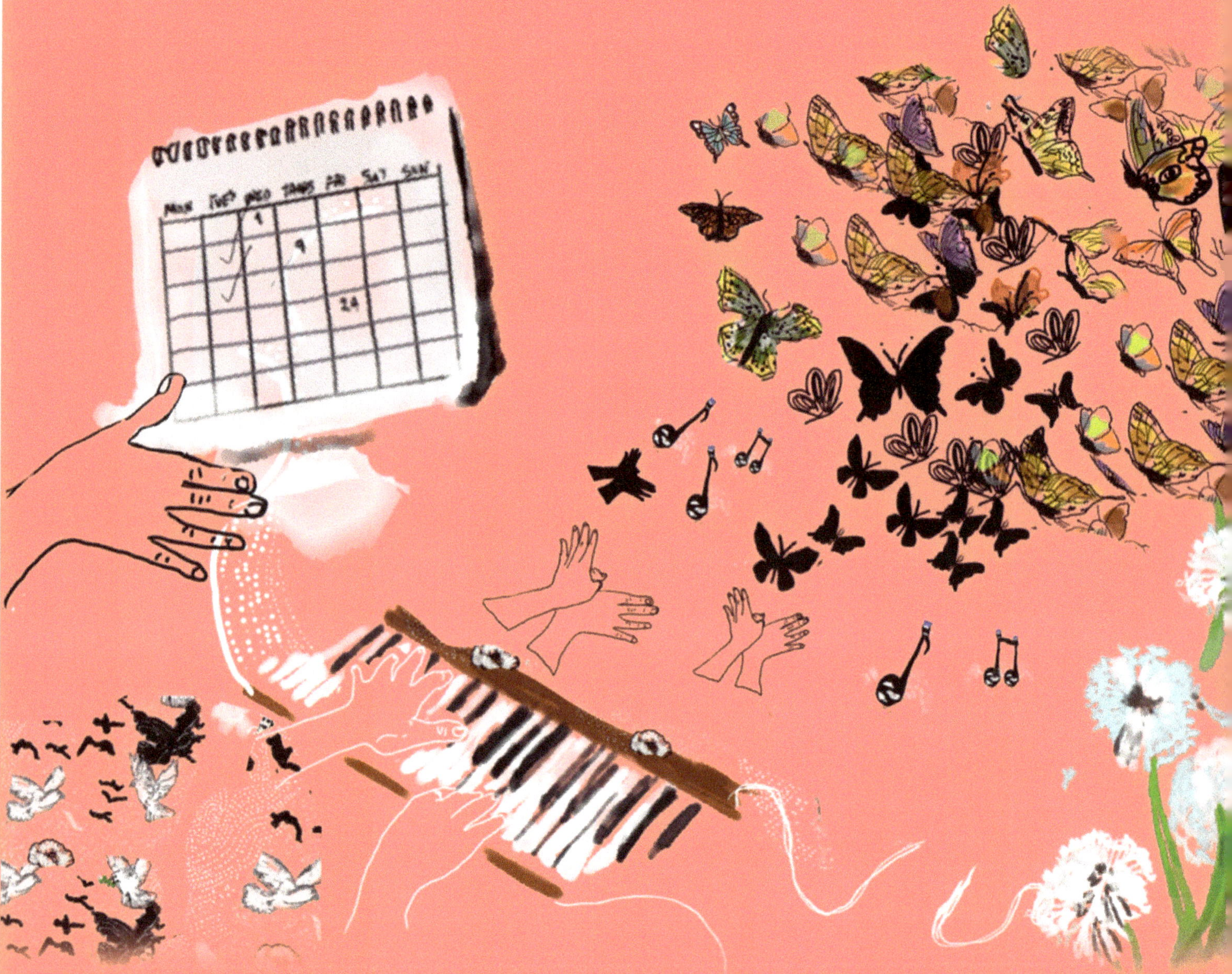

Melody goes to piano lessons for an hour every Tuesday. During the week, she plays and practices the new songs she was taught. As a dedicated music student, she listens to what her piano teacher says to become better at playing the piano.

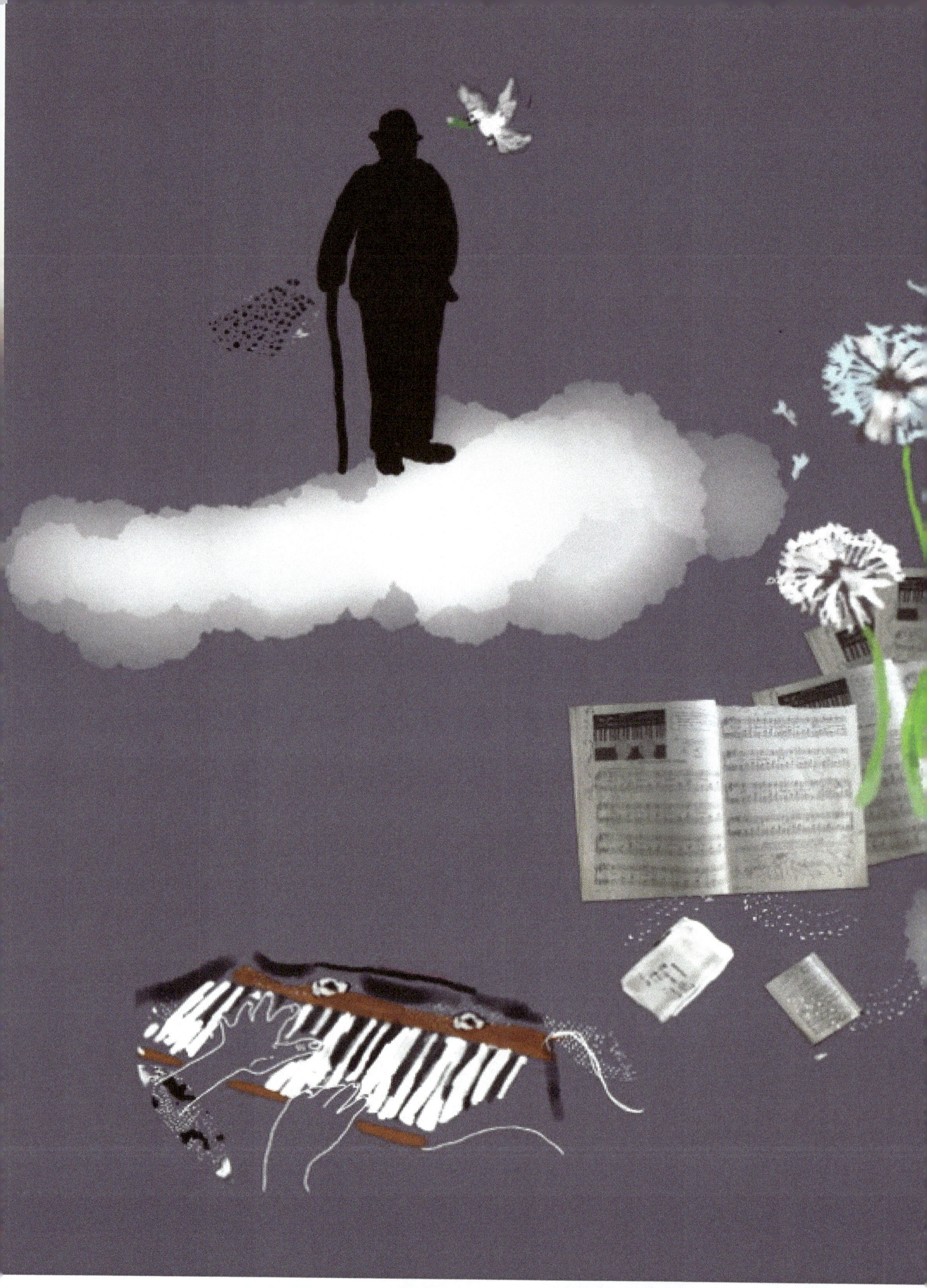

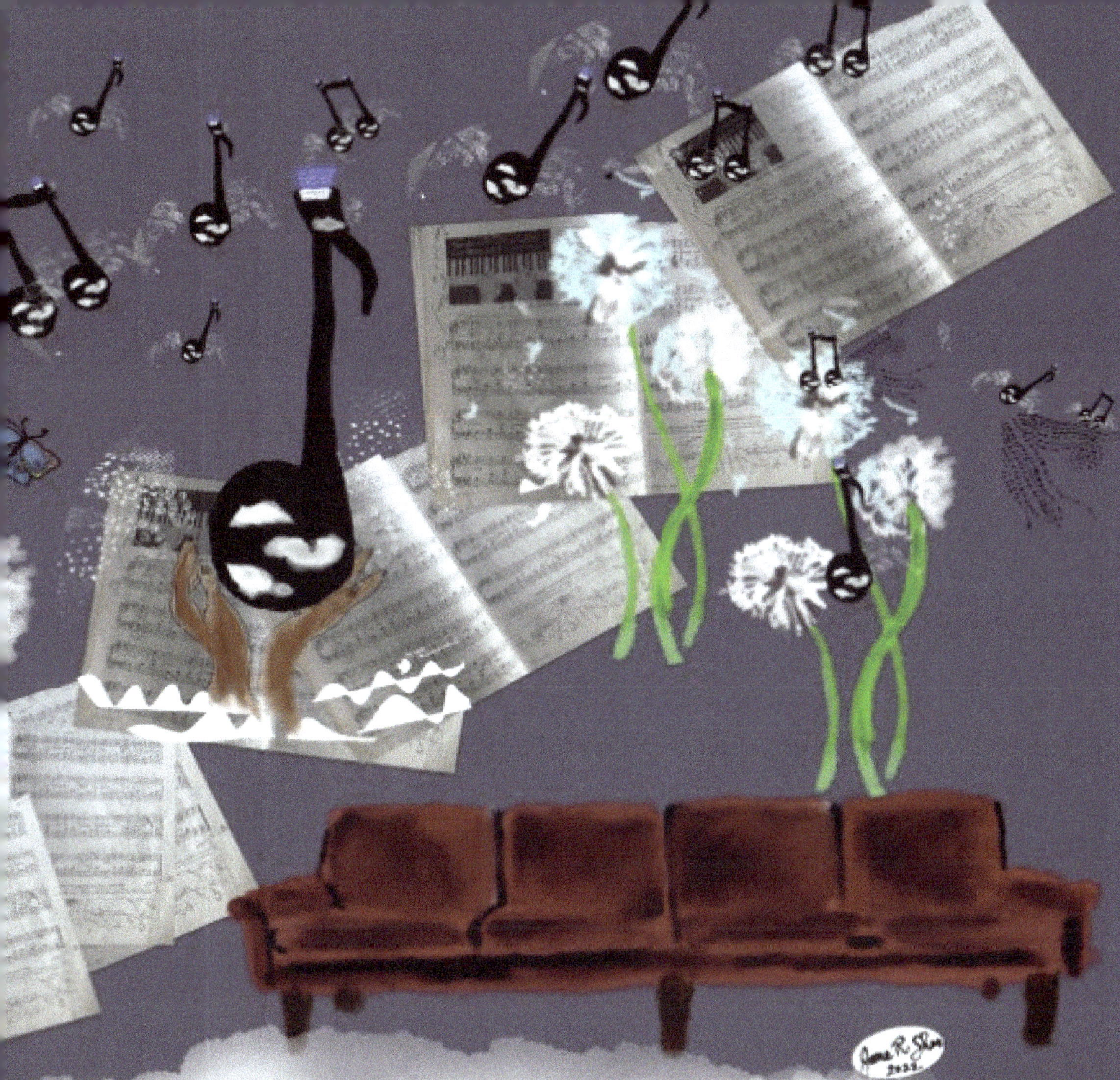

The piano she has at her house is one her grandfather purchased a long time ago when he first came to the United States. This upright, mahogany piano is sentimental because it reminds Melody of her grandfather who passed away. And when she plays, she imagines him listening intently and joyously on the corner of the burgundy couch.

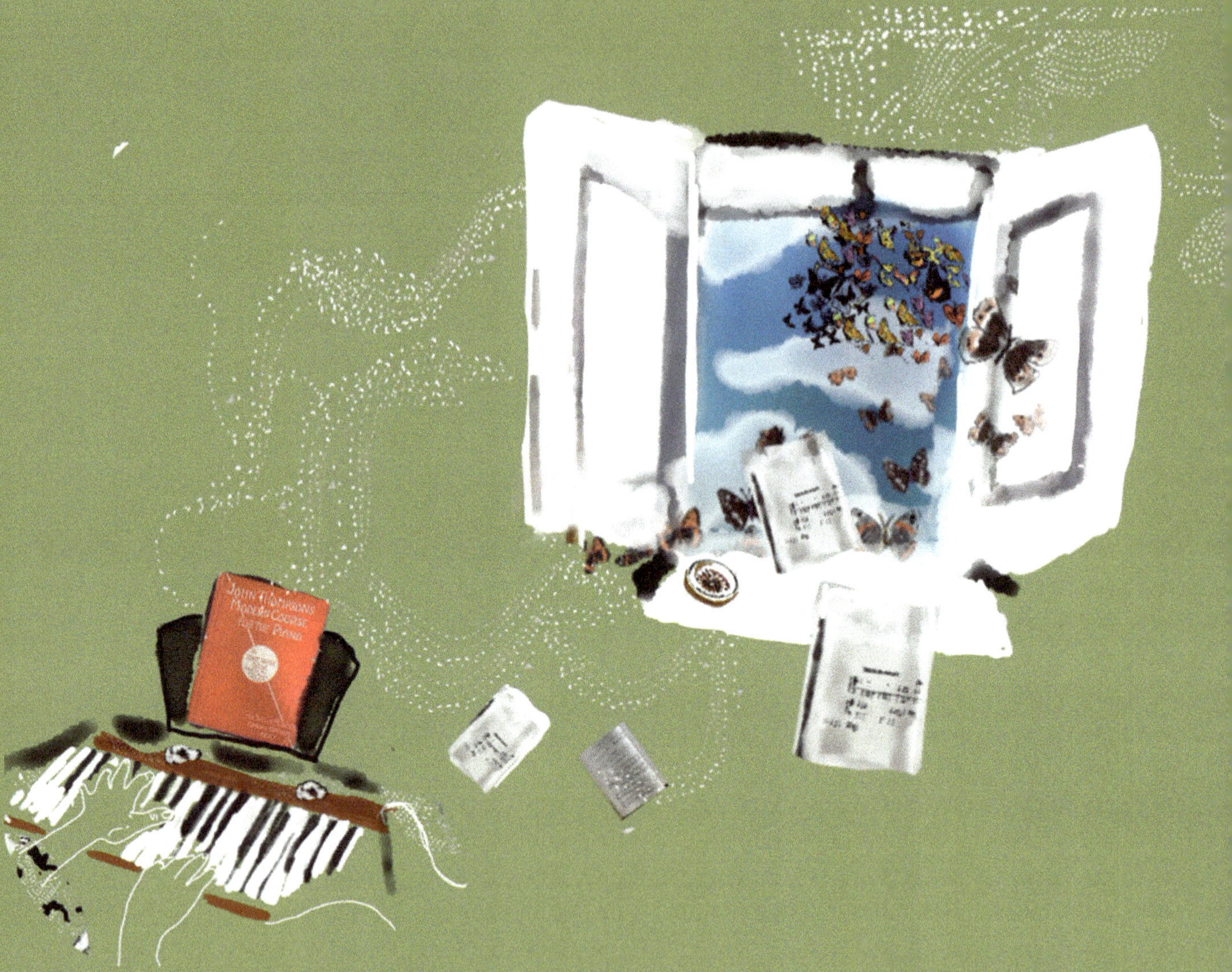

One warm April day, Melody was practicing a song for the Spring Recital at Lincoln Center in a few weeks. As she was playing, a sudden gust of wind swirled in from the open terrace window of the apartment. Her piano book crashed onto the floor and some of the music pages flew out the window. Melody was devastated. She lost the song pages for her spring recital.

" What am I going to do?" she said.

"I don't know the song well enough! I still need to keep practicing to perform in front of my piano teacher, friends, and family."

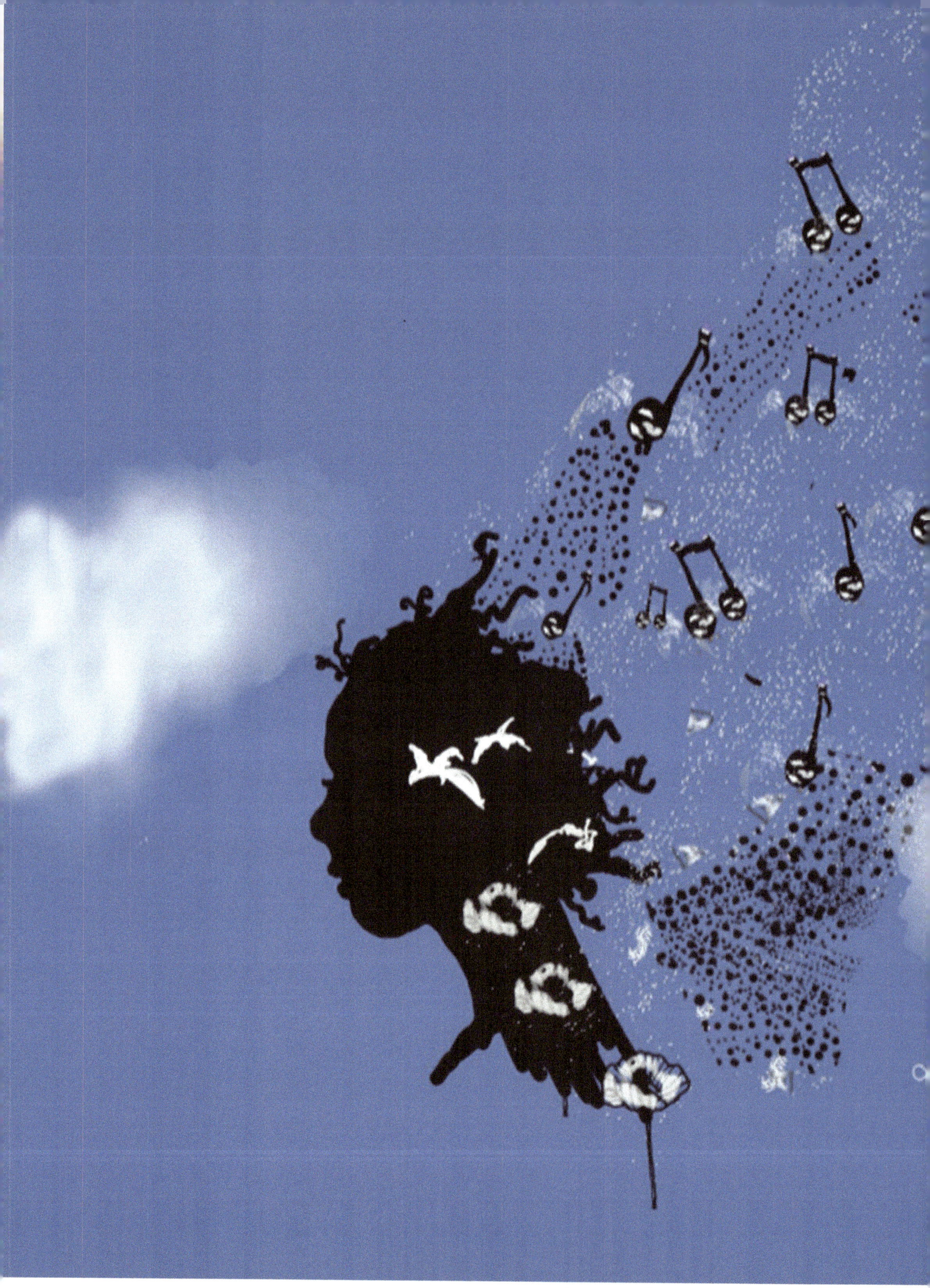

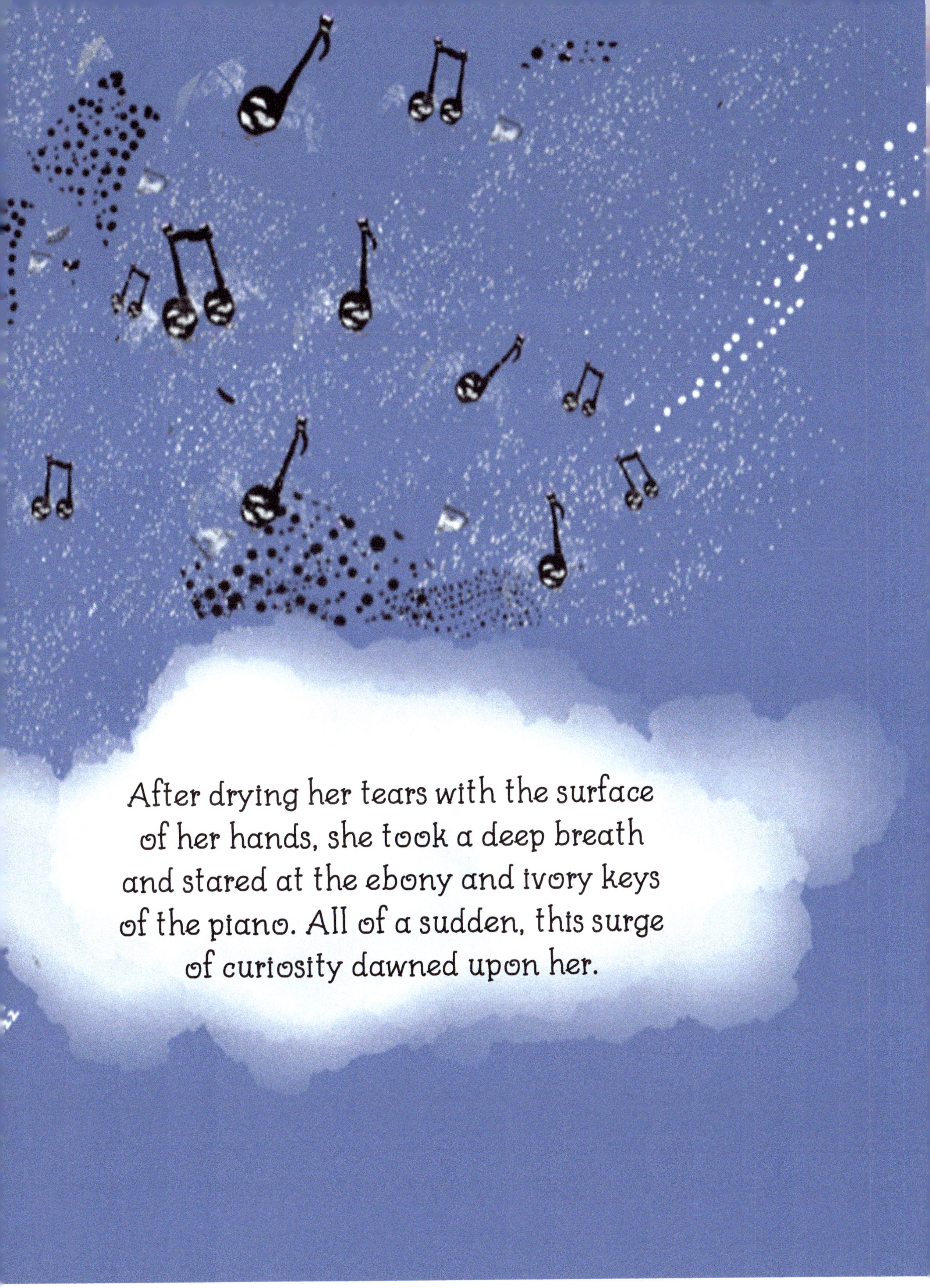

After drying her tears with the surface of her hands, she took a deep breath and stared at the ebony and ivory keys of the piano. All of a sudden, this surge of curiosity dawned upon her.

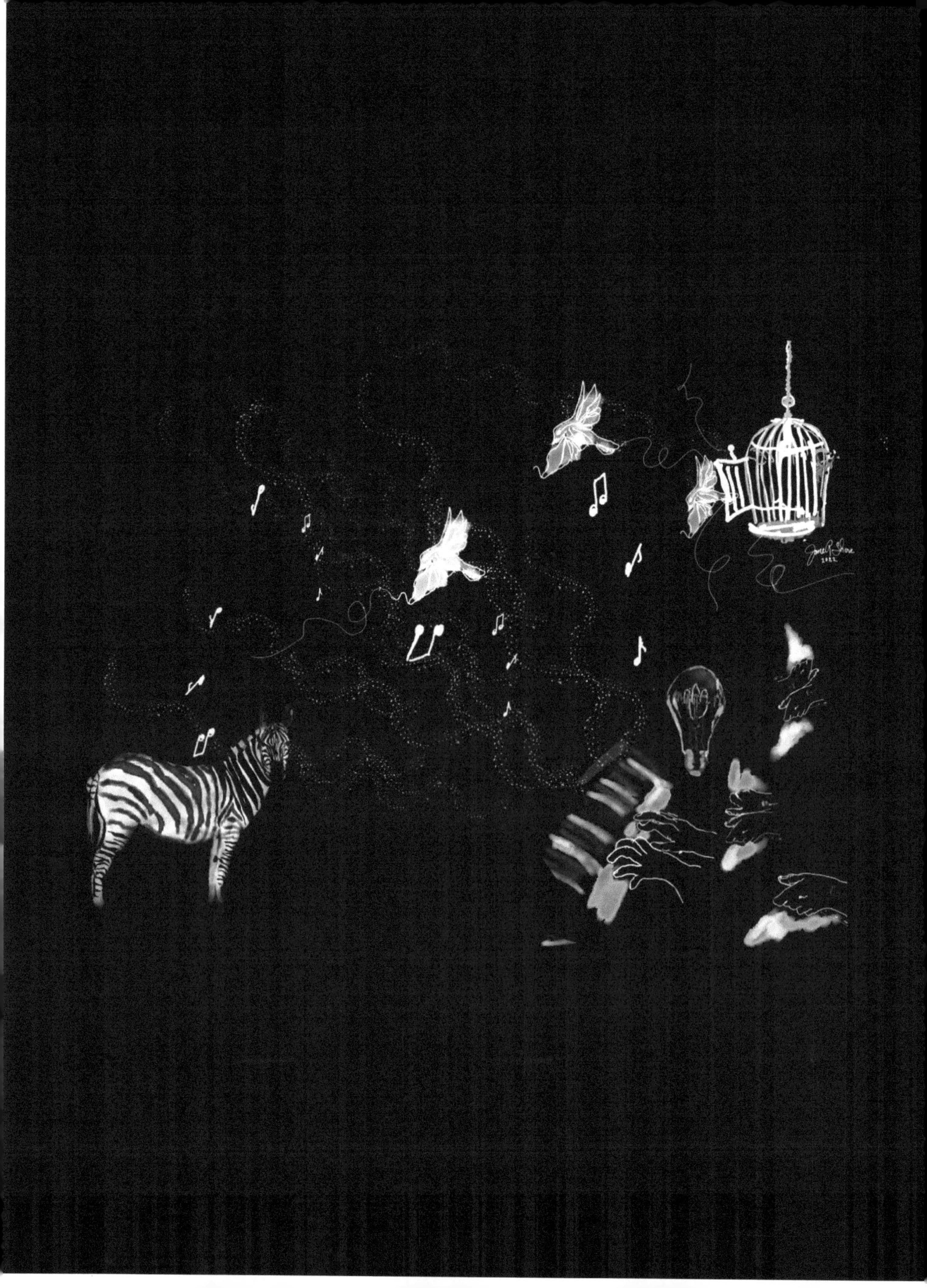

Melody wanted to explore the sounds
of the piano without her music book.
With one finger, she gently tapped a few keys.
Then with the same hand,
she started to play chords.

Moments later, Melody used her other
hand to play connected sound patterns
with the keys. These sounds soothed her
and helped bring a smile back on her face.

All of a sudden, she made the most
beautiful music on the piano—nothing
like she ever played before. She created
her very own melody—her very own
impromptu, improvised song.

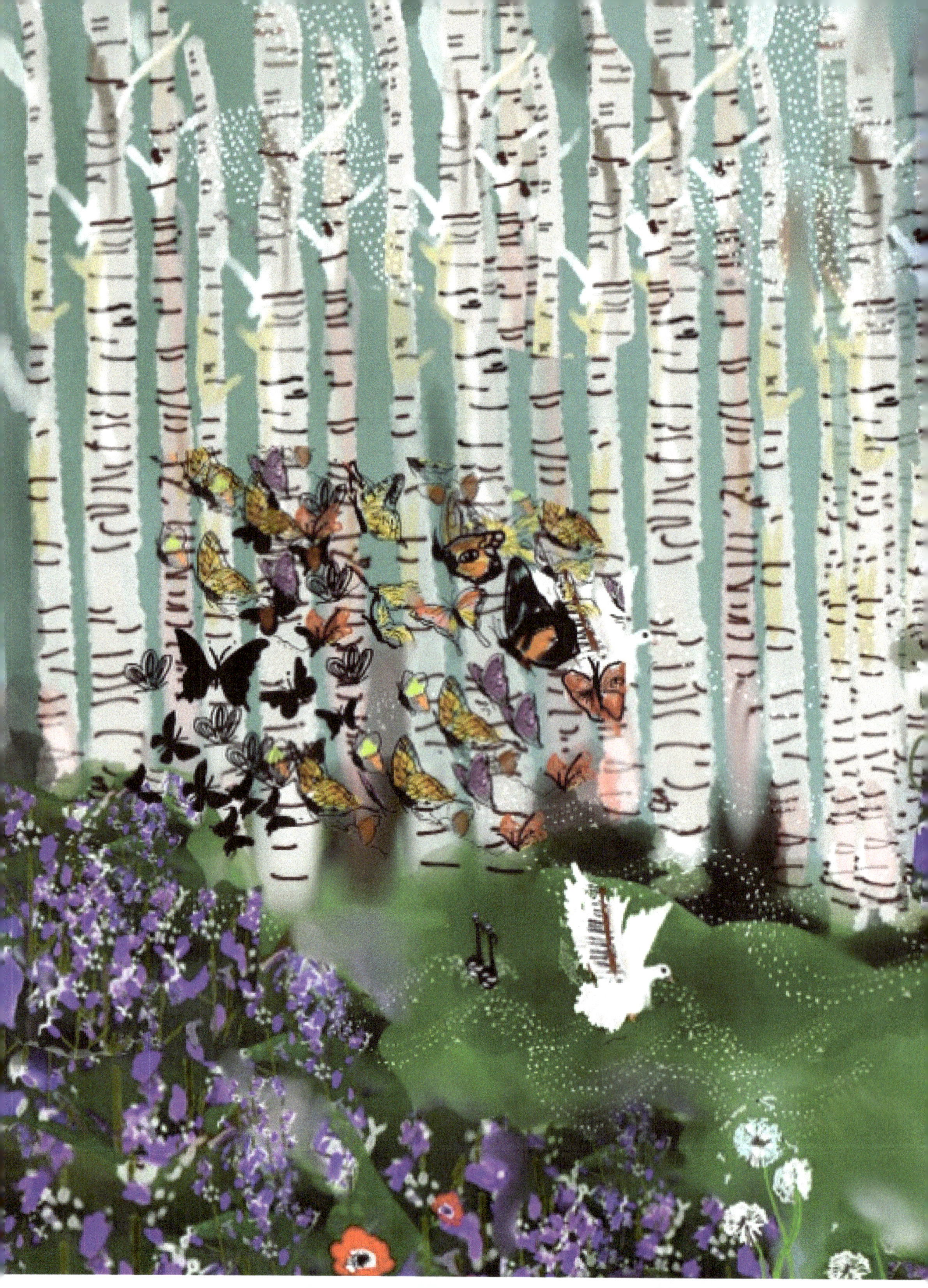

As she was playing the piano, her imagination took over. In her mind, she was in a forest collecting fragrant bluebells in a basket. While gathering her bouquet, she stopped by a flowing stream where monarch butterflies and gigantic dragonflies hovered over the mossy grounds. As this film was streaming in her imagination, Melody kept playing the piano as background music. It was as if she traveled upon a black music note and glided away to this enchanted place in her mind—a mystical land where nature inspires song and song is inspired by nature.

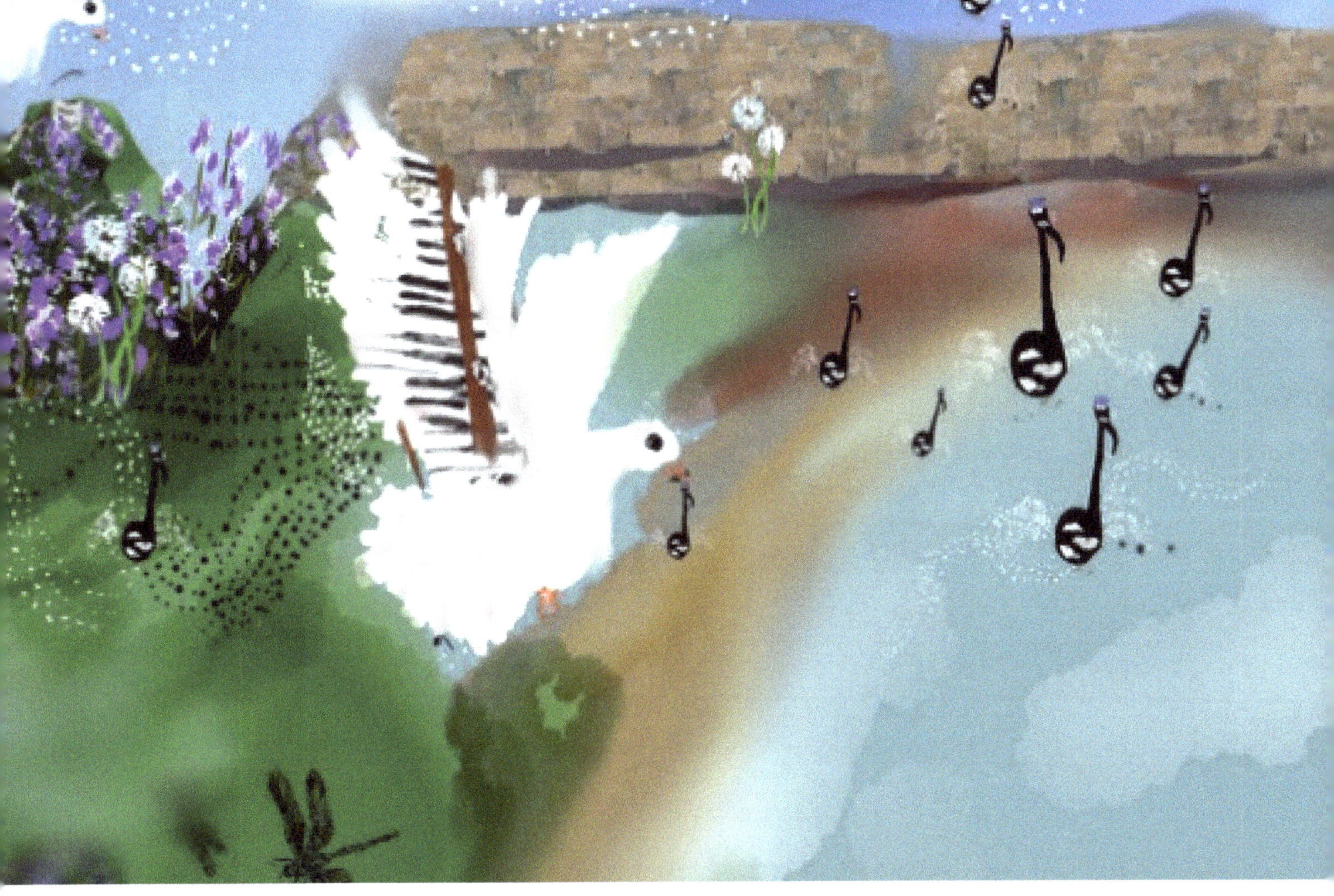

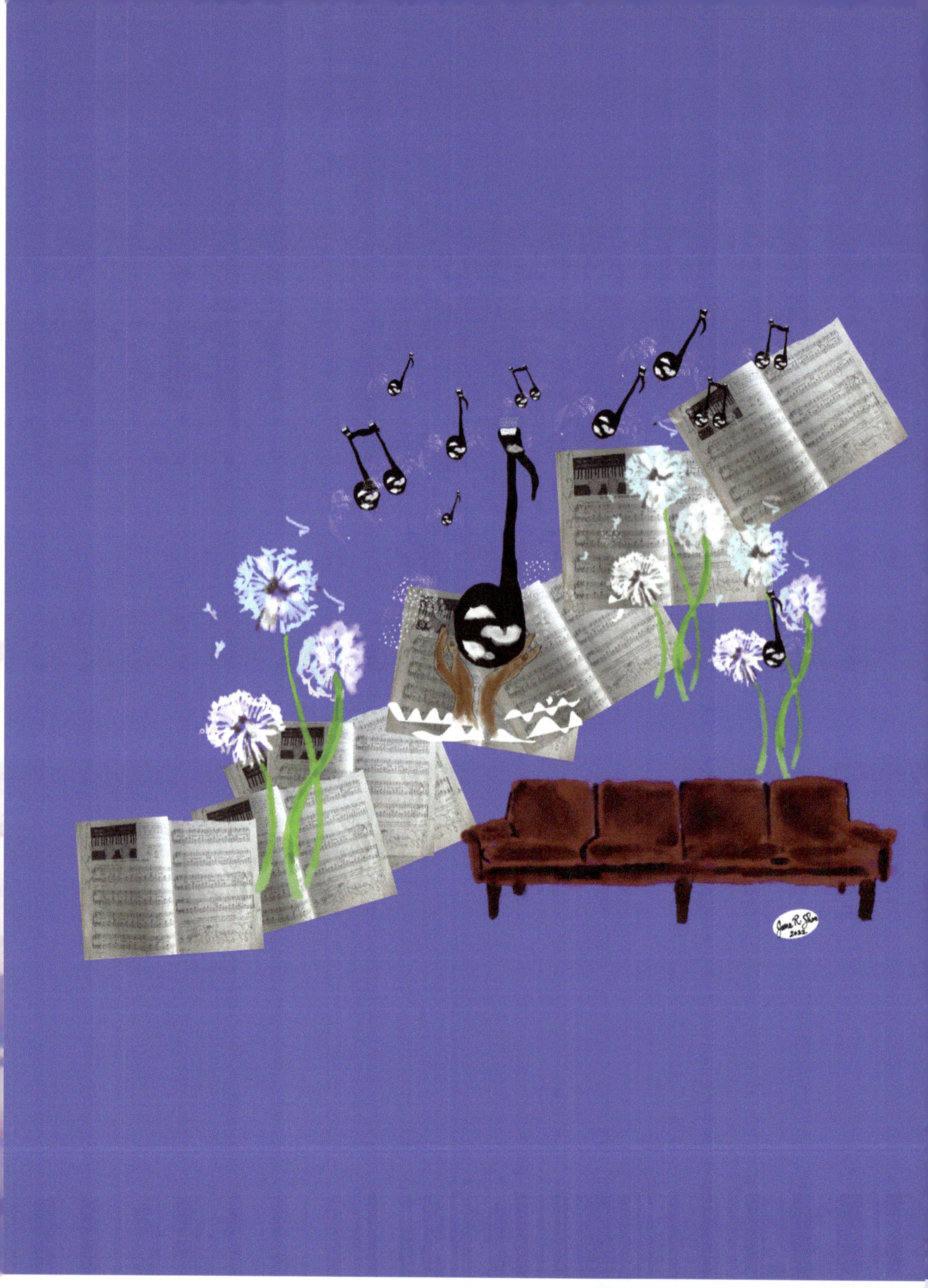

Once her fingers began to tire,
Melody began to slow down playing until
there was silence. She could not believe what
an impassioned experience she just had.
Again, she imagined her grandfather
listening intently and joyously on the
corner of the burgundy couch while
enthusiastically applauding her courageous
creation—her music, her song. It was
something no one else has ever played—
something no one else has ever heard.
This was true magic in acoustic form.

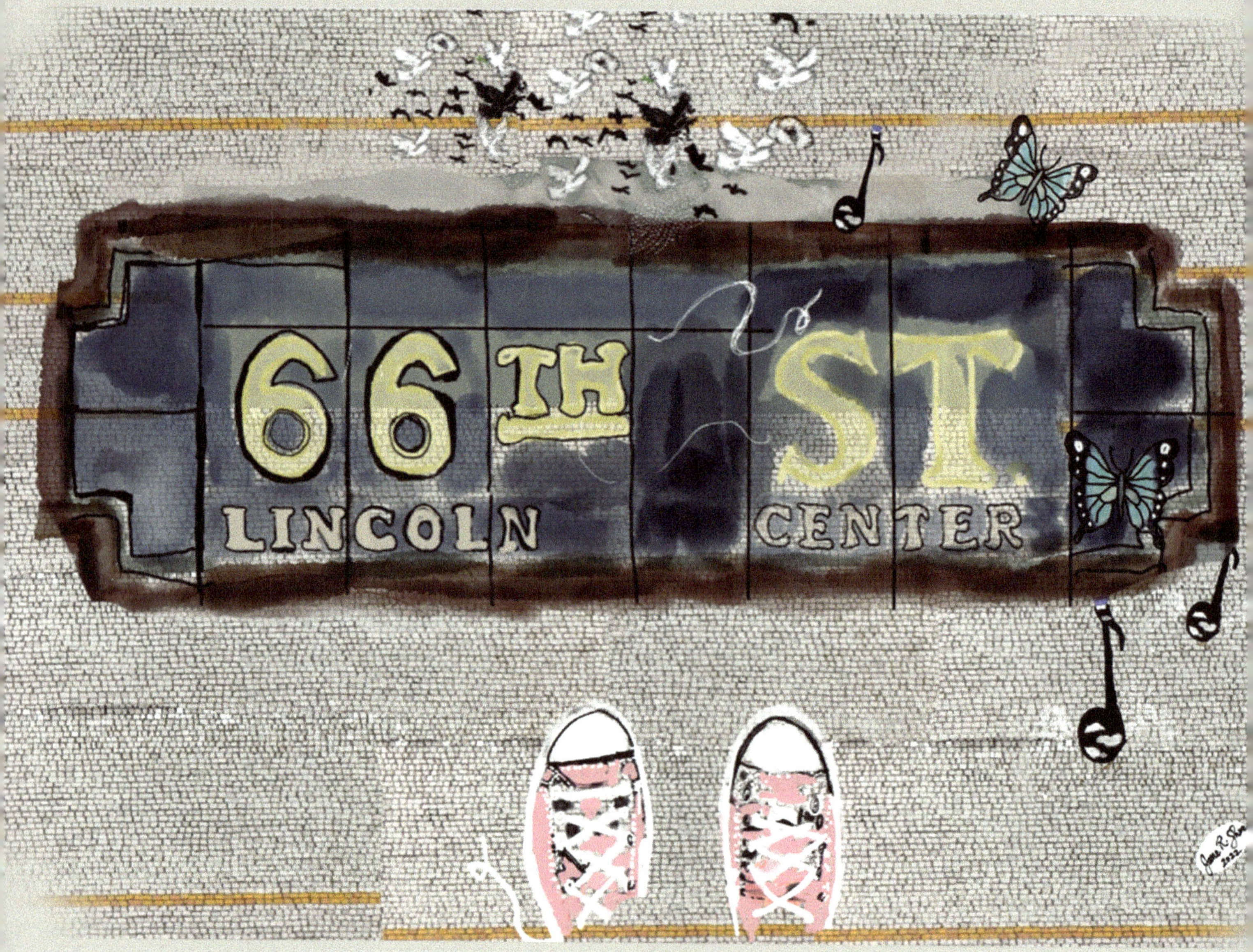
66TH ST.
LINCOLN CENTER

A few weeks later, Melody had her spring piano recital on stage at Lincoln Center with the eyes of her piano teacher, friends, and family awaiting in attention for her performance. Once Melody played a song from her music book, she surprised everyone with the song she created the time her music pages flew away.

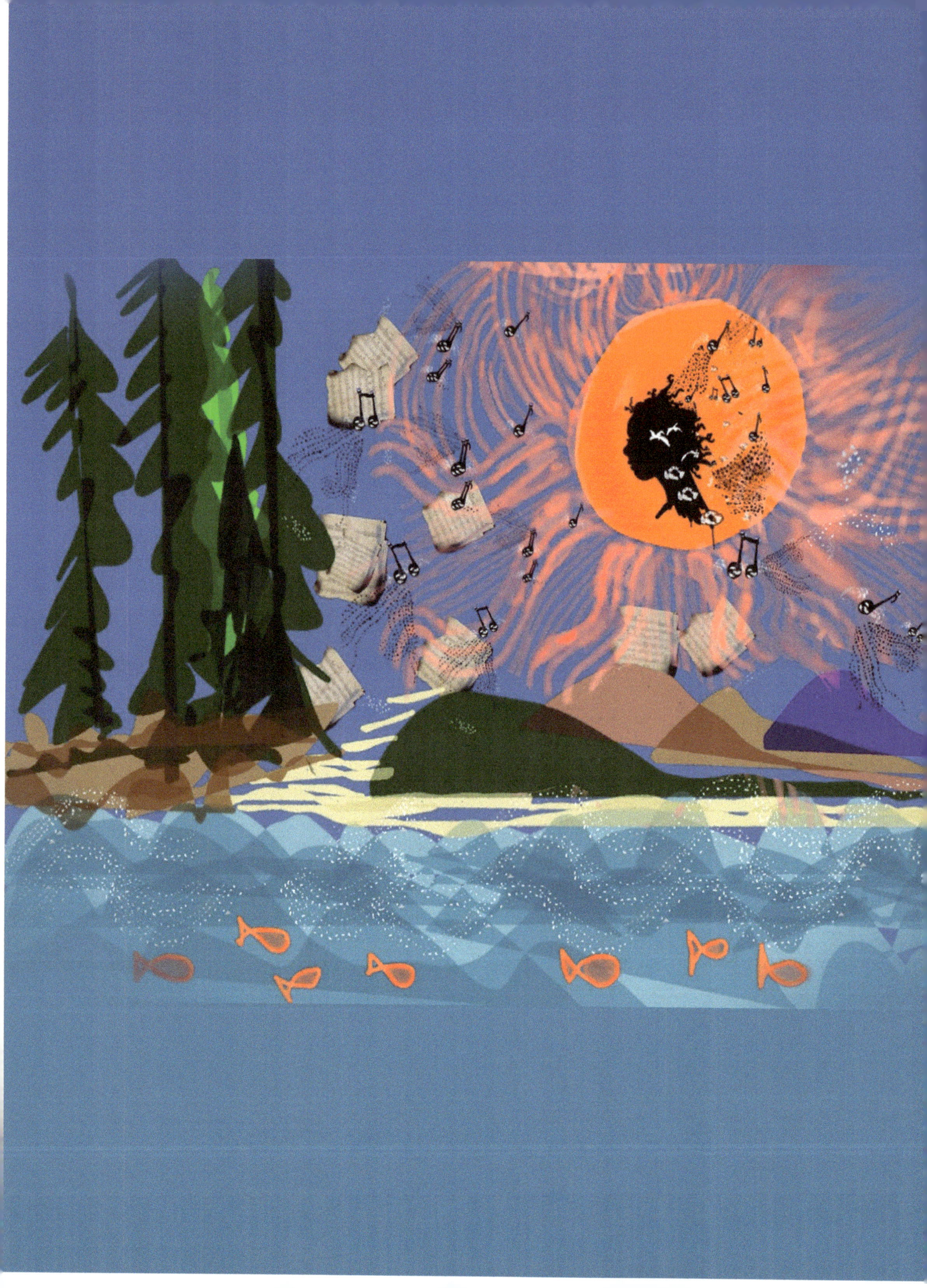

As Melody played her original tune,
she was transported once again to
that enchanted forest in her mind.
Her piano teacher, friends, and family
watched and heard her music with awe.
They could not believe the beautiful sounds
Melody had created on the piano.
Once she finished the song, everyone in
the audience stood up for
a standing ovation.

"Encore, Encore," they all bellowed!

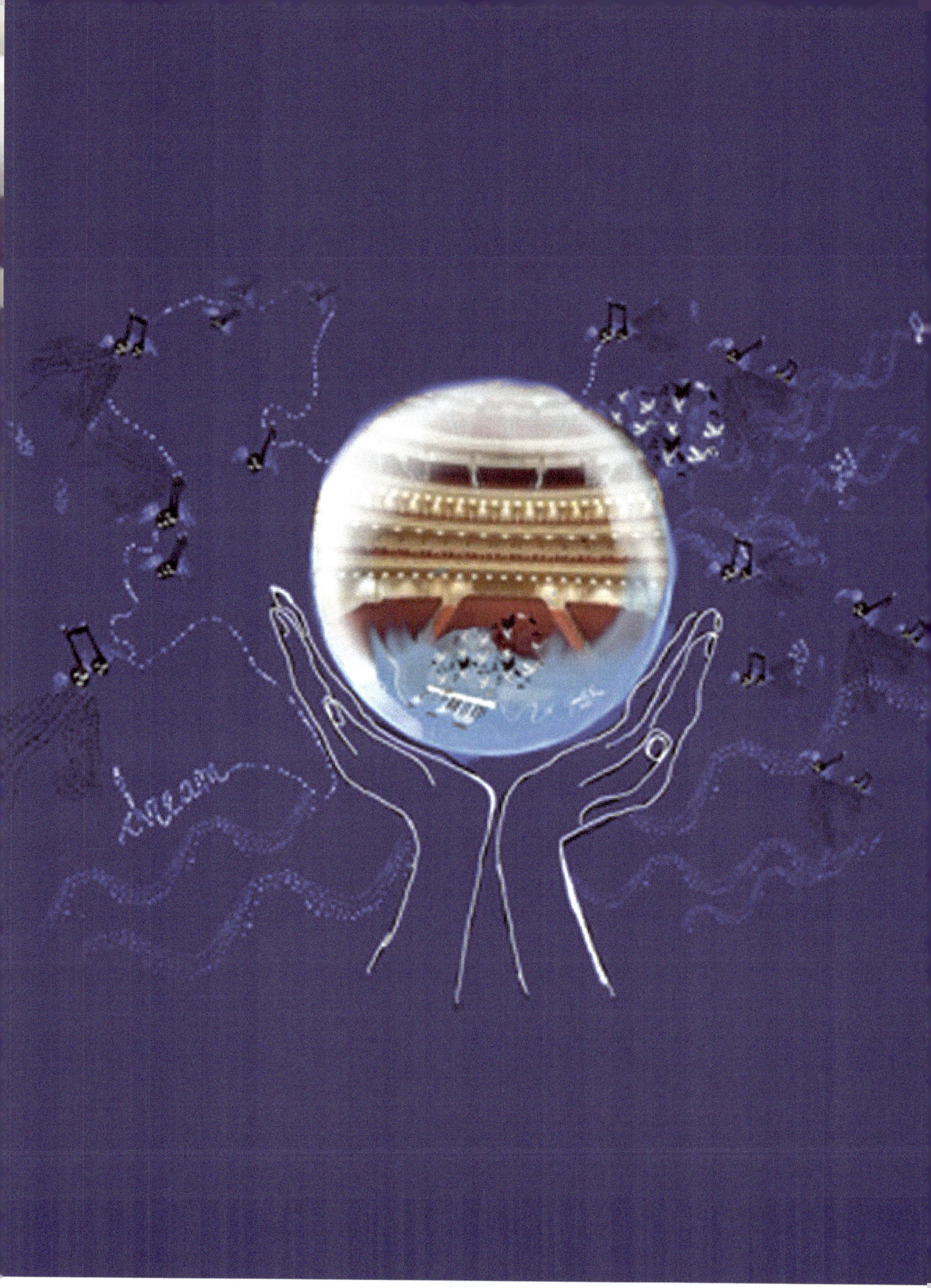
dream

Melody humbly bowed and smiled, then slowly gazed at the back of the audience where she imagined her grandfather clapping enthusiastically again, watching intently and joyously. Melody felt proud to share her music with the world. And it all began with an unexpected spark of curiosity.

10620 Treena Street, Suite 230
San Diego, California,
CA 92131 USA
www.readersmagnet.com
1.619.354.2643

www.ingramcontent.com/pod-product-compliance
Ingram Content Group UK Ltd.
Pitfield, Milton Keynes, MK11 3LW, UK
UKHW062002290726
14090UKWH00021B/1349